Printed in the USA
CPSIA information can be obtained
at www.ICGtesting.com
JSHW060047150824
68134JS00031B/2666

זְמַן לִקְרֹא

TIME TO READ
HEBREW
ACTIVITY
BOOK

FOR VOLUMES
ONE & TWO

REVIEW & ENRICHMENT

**Hillary Zana
and Dina Maiben**

A.R.E. Publishing, Inc.
an imprint of
Behrman House, Inc
Millburn, NJ

TO THE TEACHER

The זְמַן לִקְרֹא Activity Book supplements זְמַן לִקְרֹא Volumes One and Two. The Activity Book provides:
- Review activities for students to do after vacations or as homework.
- Remediation activities for students who score below 8 out of 10 on the lesson evaluations.
- Enrichment activities to challenge more advanced students.

It is not necessary for each student to complete every page. Assign enrichment pages to students who have finished a lesson in the זְמַן לִקְרֹא Workbook before the rest of the class. Have a group of slower students do a reading review page with the teacher, while another group plays a reading game from this Activity Book.

SPECIFIC SKILLS

The worksheets in this Activity Book provide additional practice in the following areas:
- Phonetic Reading
- Text Reading from the Siddur, Torah, and Haggadah
- Key Word Review
- Vocabulary
- Alef-Bet Order
- Writing in Script

Reading Pages (such as pages 4, 38, and 44) have been designed for review or remediation of reading problems. It is important that students do not attempt to read these pages independently. Some of these pages deal with a specific problem common to a particular lesson (e.g., page 44). Others simply provide more decoding practice in a varied format (e.g., page 9). In either case, if students read to themselves, mistakes may be reinforced and certainly will not be remediated. Teachers may choose to use these pages with the entire class, especially for review purposes. Alternately, students could read to a peer tutor, an older student, or an aide while the teacher moves from pair to pair, monitoring their progress. By contrast, phonetic activity pages (such as pages 3, 11, and 49) may be assigned for independent seat work or as homework.

If there is a group that requires remediation, an excellent option is for the teacher to work with these students while the rest of the class is involved in a different activity. In this case, the teacher should deal directly with the problem area, re-teaching as necessary using the felt board, foam letters, or flash cards, and then using this Activity Book for reading practice. In this way, students avoid the need to repeat reading a page in the Workbook, an experience that many students find to be negative.

A final method of using the phonetic Reading Pages is to send this Activity Book home and have a knowledgeable family member listen to the child read. Do not, however, count on family members to remediate reading problems.

As students gain mastery of phonetic decoding skills, the teacher may wish to challenge them with reading texts of increasing length and difficulty. Pages 71-78 provide various texts from the Siddur, Haggadah, and Torah that contain the specific reading items taught in lessons 18-20.

In addition to phonetic decoding practice, many pages in this Activity Book are designed to supplement the vocabulary and beginning language skills introduced in the Workbooks. It should be noted that the vocabulary pages are designed to provide additional practice for students who are completing the language component of the program. They should not be used as introductory material for Hebrew language. Some of these vocabulary pages enrich the optional language component by providing a limited amount of new material.

Before using any page in this זְמַן לִקְרֹא Activity Book, assemble the materials needed e.g., pencils, plain paper, markers, highlighters, crayons, scissors, game tokens (such as beans, coins, or plastic chips), index cards, stapler, hole punch, narrow ribbon, etc.

Many of the pages in this Activity Book are in game format. Students may play these games with a partner or small group. A few students may play a game while the rest are working independently or with the teacher in one of the זְמַן לִקְרֹא Workbooks or on another page in this Activity Book. Another option is to play a game with the entire class using teams. In this case, you may want to make an overhead transparency of the game so that everyone can follow along together.

The concluding pages of this Activity Book are devoted to writing in Hebrew script. They should be used only after students have completed the זְמַן לִקְרֹא Workbooks. Students are asked to write in block letters throughout the Workbooks and this Activity Book in order to reinforce the shapes of the letters that they are learning to read. However, students who go on to study the Hebrew language will find script a more convenient way to write.

This זְמַן לִקְרֹא Activity Book will help students drill Hebrew reading in an enjoyable manner. Decoding is a mechanical skill. However, it is the first step in developing Hebrew literacy, a crucial aspect of what — hopefully — will be a lifetime of positive Jewish experiences for our students.

Lesson 1
KEY WORD:
שַׁבָּת

HIDDEN PICTURE

Color yellow all the spaces that have the sound of "AH".

Color brown all the spaces that have the sound of "B".

Color purple all the spaces that have the sound of "SH".

Leave white all the spaces that have the sound of "T".

Color green all the spaces that have any other sound.

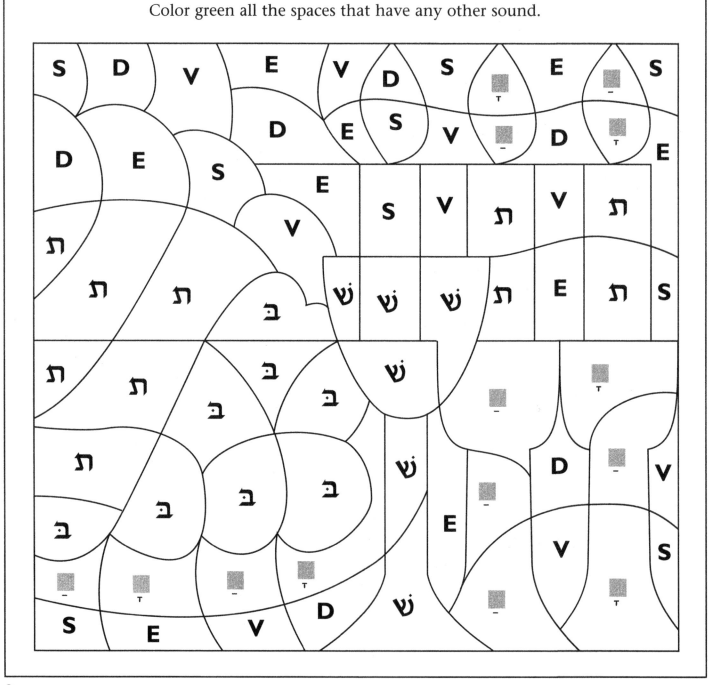

PRACTICE MAKES PERFECT

Read the following:

שֵׁשׁ	שָׁשׁ	בֵּב	בַּב	1.
בֵּשׁ בָּשׁ	בָּשׁ	שֵׁת	שָׁת	2.
בֵּת בָּת	בָּת	שֵׁב	שָׁב	3.

Decorate your שַׁבָּת table. Read the sounds in each flower.

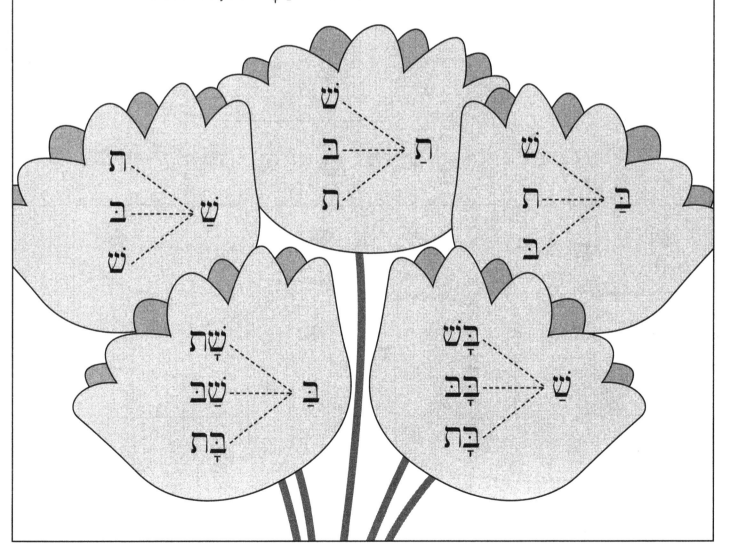

4

Lesson 2
KEY WORD:
דָג

FEED THE FISH

Read the following words. Then write each one in the correct fish below.

בַּד	תַ	תָ	דְ
גַת	דָג	תַג	דַב
בֶּגֶד	שָׁגָת	שָׁגָת	שָׁבָד
שָׁגָד	שָׁבָת	בָּדָשׁ	שָׁתַג

Words that have the sound of "D"

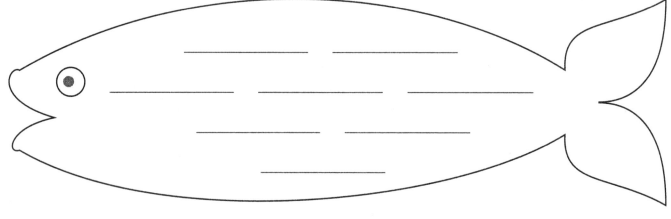

Words that have the sound of "T"

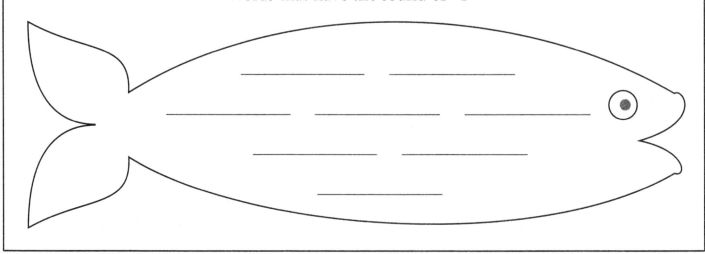

5

Lesson 2
KEY WORD:
דָּג

FOUR IN A ROW

Play this game with a partner. One player is "X", the other is "O".
Take turns reading the Hebrew in any box below. If you read
correctly, mark that box with your X or O. The first to get four
boxes in a straight line in any direction is the winner.

שָׁדָת	גַּג	דָּת	גַּת	דְּשׁ	שָׁגַג
בָּדָת	שָׁד	בַּגַּג	גְ	גַּד	בַּב
דָּת	תָּדְשׁ	גַּב	דַּדַב	דָּג	דַּשׁ
תַּגַד	שַׁבָּת	שָׁשׁ	דַּגַת	דַּב	בַּבַג
דָּג	דַּ	בַּתָּג	גָּשׁ	בַּת	דַּגְשׁ
בַּתָּ	תַּד	שָׁג	גַּשׁ	בָּגַשׁ	שָׁדָג

6

MAKE YOUR MARK

Use a yellow marker or crayon.

1. Color the vowels in the words below that make the "**ee**" sound.
2. Read all the vowel sounds to your teacher or partner.
3. Then read the words.

בְּד	גְּד	תְּשׁ	אַשׁ	גְּשׁ
אַד	מְד	מָשׁ	דְּשׁ	בְּשׁ
תָּאֵד	גְּמָד	דַּמְשׁ	תְּדְשׁ	תַּבְּשׁ
גְּאֵד	תָּמְד	גְּמַשׁ	אָדְשׁ	אַבְּשׁ

Now read the following combinations.

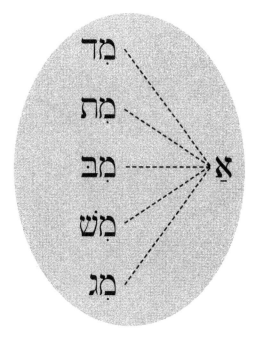

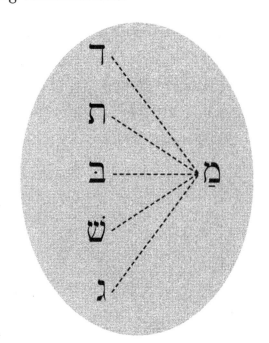

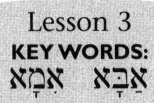

Lesson 3
KEY WORDS:
אַבָּא אִמָּא

VOWEL HINTS

When you go for a checkup, the doctor asks you
to open your mouth and say "Ah."
Then the doctor puts a stick in your mouth.

When you see the Hebrew vowel that is shaped like a stick
(or a stick with a handle), remember to say "Ah."

Write the two vowels that make the "**ah**" sound on the
picture of the stick above. Then read these words to a friend.

שַׁבָּת   בַּת   דָּג   אַבָּא   שֶׁמֶשׁ

The ◼ makes the sound of "**ee**".
It looks like a little round b**ea**d.
Write the Hebrew vowel that
makes the "**ee**" sound under the
box in the big bead.

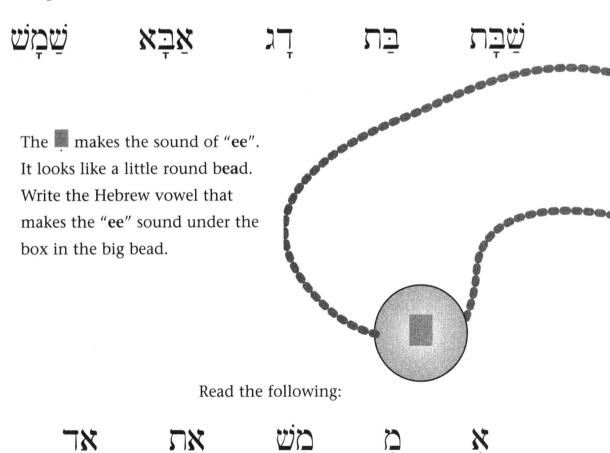

Read the following:

אִ   מִ   מִשׁ   אִת   אִד

8

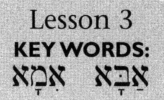

Lesson 3
KEY WORDS:
אַבָּא אִמָּא

DON'T LET THE BUBBLES POP!

Read the sounds in each soap bubble to your teacher.

KEY WORDS:

מַצָּה הַגָּדָה

CLIMB THE PYRAMID

Egypt is the land where the Hebrews were slaves to Pharaoh. It is also known for its ancient pyramids in which the Pharaohs were buried. Start in the lower right corner of the pyramid and read the words in each row to your teacher or to a friend. If you make a mistake, start over again. Keep trying until you can "climb" the pyramid without making a mistake.

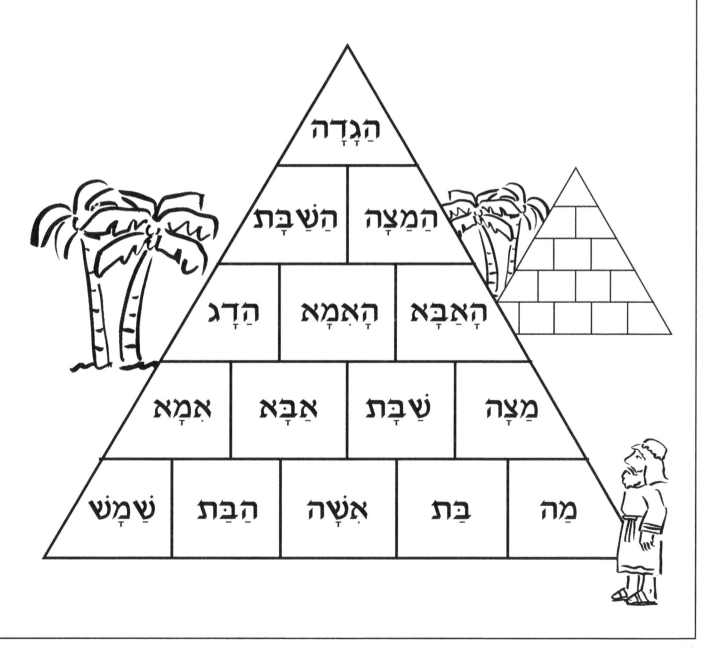

הַגָּדָה

הַשַּׁבָּת הַמַּצָּה

הַדָּג הָאִמָּא הָאַבָּא

אִמָּא אַבָּא שַׁבָּת מַצָּה

שֶׁמֶשׁ הַבַּת אִשָּׁה בַּת מַה

Lesson 4
KEY WORDS:
מַצָּה הַגָּדָה

MATZAH MAZE

It's the night of the Seder and the מַצָּה is hidden somewhere in the house. Start in the attic. Read each word correctly to your teacher or partner as you go through the maze. Circle the word מַצָּה when you find it.

START

הִצָּה הַגָּדַת	בַּת	בָּא	הַגָּדָה
צָמְה הַשֶּׁמֶשׁ	הַדָּג	הַשַּׁבָּת	צָמֵא
מַצַּת בָּאָה	אִמָא	הָאִמָא	בָּה
מִצָּה אַבָּא	שֶׁמֶשׁ	מַצַּת	מַה
אַתָּה מַצָּה	צָמְה	מִצַּת	צָמַד

11

Lesson 5

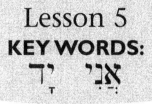

KEY WORDS:
אֲנִי יָד

THE YELLOW YUD

The letter **י** can be tricky. Sometimes it sounds like the consonant **Y**. At other times, it is part of a vowel sound. How can you tell which sound the **י** makes? Here is the rule:

> If the letter **י** has a vowel sound after it, then it is a consonant. Example: יָד

Color with a yellow marker or crayon the letters below that make the consonant "Y" sound. Then read all the words.

יָד   אֲנִי

בַּיִת   מִי   מַיָה

יַגִּיד   בִּינָה   צַיִד

דָּנִי   תַּיִשׁ   מִיָד

צִיצִית

אִישׁ

12

Lesson 5
KEY WORDS:
אֲנִי יָד

GIVE A HAND

In each finger there is a word. Each word has a sound-alike in the palm of the hand. Write the correct sound-alike on the line in each finger.

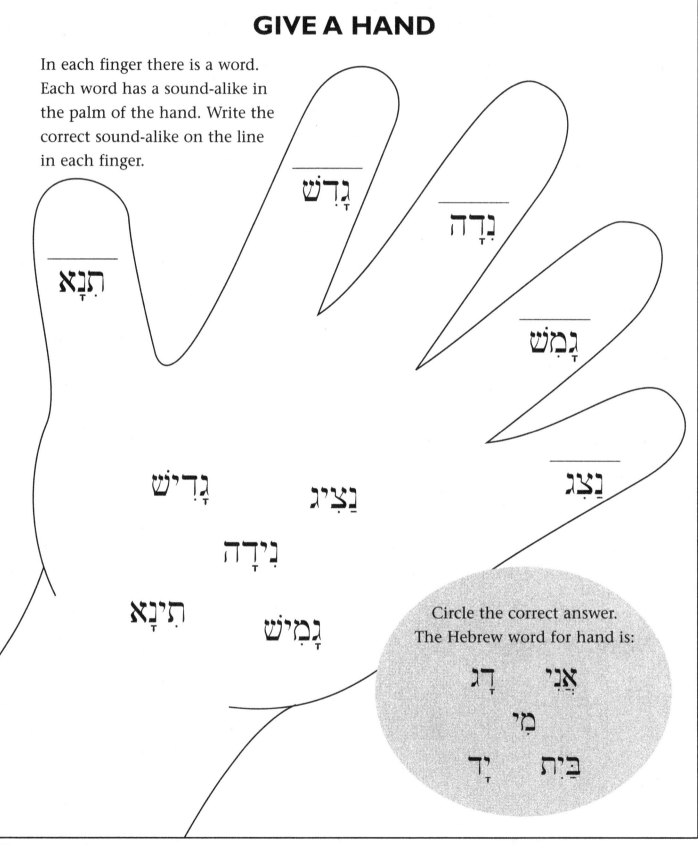

גְּדַשׁ

נָדָה

תְּנָא

גָּמֹשׁ

נַצֵג

גְּדִישׁ   נַצִיג

נִידָה

תִּינָא   גָּמִישׁ

Circle the correct answer. The Hebrew word for hand is:

אֲנִי   דָג

מִי

בַּיִת   יָד

13

Lesson 5

אֲנִי   יָד

FIND YOUR WAY HOME

Play this game with a friend. You will need one die, and each of you will need one game marker. Take turns. Roll the die and move your marker one space for each dot. Read and translate the word you land on. If you do this correctly, stay on that spot. If not, go back to where you were. The winner is the first one to reach the בַּיִת. Use the Dictionary on page 84 of זְמַן לִקְרֹא Volume One to check your answers.

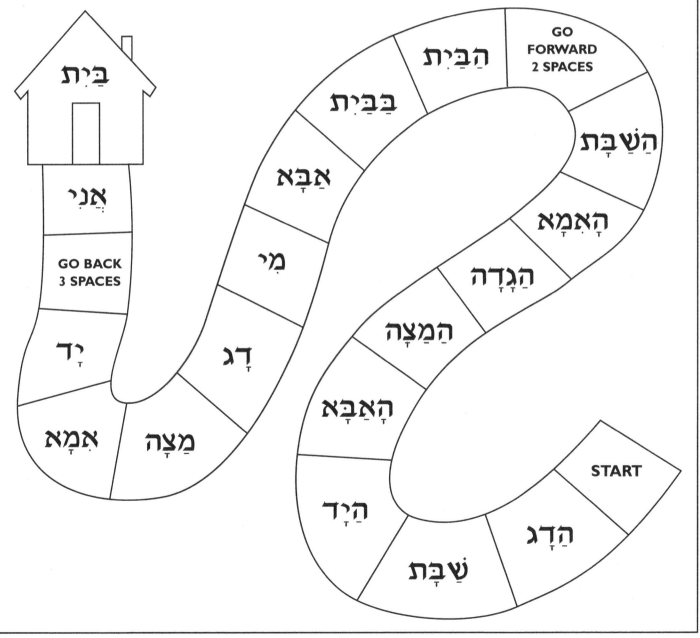

Lesson 6
KEY WORDS:
קִדּוּשׁ יַיִן

BE A WORD BUILDER

Read the following combinations:

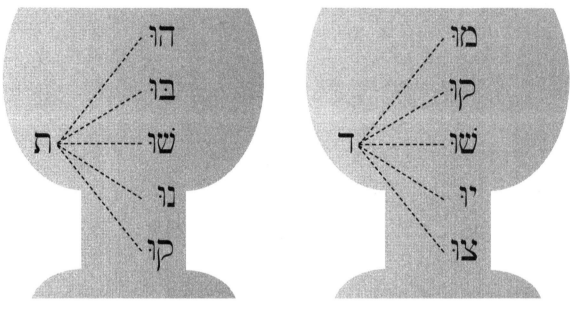

Each of the words below has more than one syllable.
Read each syllable. Then read the entire word.

בְּנוּ	=	נוּ	+	בְּ	.1
קָנוּ	=	נוּ	+	קָ	.2
הָיוּ	=	יוּ	+	הָ	.3
מִיוּן	=	יוּן	+	מִ	.4

קָדִימָה	=	מָה	+	דִי	+	קָ	.5
שָׁתִינוּ	=	נוּ	+	תִי	+	שָׁ	.6

KEY WORDS:

קָדוֹשׁ יַיִן

THUMBS UP

Use your thumb to help you read the words in the box below.

1. Cover the silent letter at the end of each word with your left thumb.
2. Read the word.
3. Uncover the silent letter.
4. Read the word again.

קָמָה	הִיא	הוּא	מִידָה	אֲנִי	1.
אַבָּא	שִׁשִׁי	דָּנִי	אִמָּא	בָּא	2.
קָנִיתִי	אֲדָמָה	אֱמִתִי	צָמָא	נוּמִי	3.

RHYME TIME

Circle the two words in each line that rhyme.

Example:  בָּא   דִין   דָן   מַה

בְּנוּ	דִינָה	בִּינָה	צִדְי	א.
שָׁנוּן	תַּנִין	גַנוֹן	שָׁמֵן	ב.
גְנוּי	אֲנִי	קָנוּי	הָיוּ	ג.

16

Lesson 6

KEY WORDS:
קָדוֹשׁ יַיִן

מַה בַּבַּיִת? מִי בַּבַּיִת?

Read each sentence.
Copy each sentence under the correct picture.

מִי בַּבַּיִת?	מַה בַּבַּיִת?
אַבָּא בַּבַּיִת.	דָג בַּבַּיִת.
אִמָּא בַּבַּיִת.	יַיִן בַּבַּיִת.
דָנִי בַּבַּיִת.	קָדוֹשׁ בַּבַּיִת.
דִינָה בַּבַּיִת.	שַׁבָּת בַּבַּיִת.

_____ _____ _____

_____ _____ _____

_____

Lesson 7
KEY WORD:
פּוּרִים

FILL THE BASKET

It is a lovely פּוּרִים custom to send gifts of food and drink to your friends. These פּוּרִים gifts are called Mishloach Manot. Help דָּן and רוּת prepare a Mishloach Manot basket for their friends. Circle the food and drink items on the list on the right that might go in a פּוּרִים basket. Then, fill the basket by drawing in the food and drink items that you have chosen.

Shopping List

הַגָּדָה	יַיִן
מַיִם	פִּיתָה
פִּיצָה	גִּיר
דָּג	בַּנָנָה
מַצָה	יָד

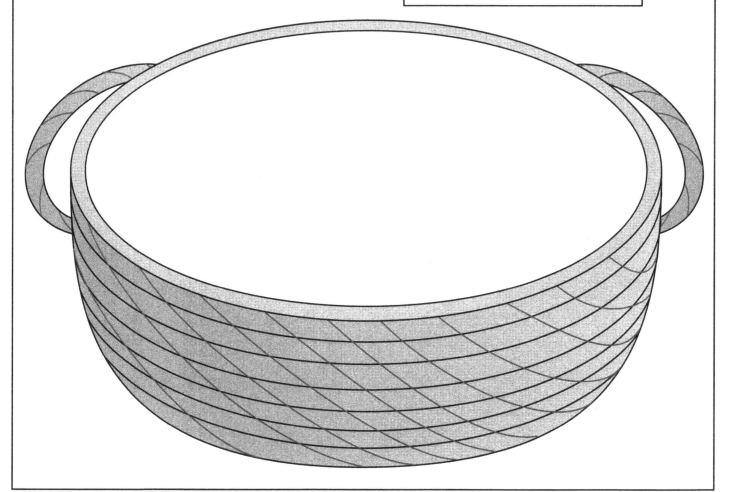

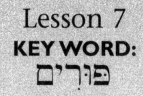

פּוּרִים

Read the words on the Megillah.
Cross out wicked Haman's name.

בּוּ הָמָן!

פּ
וּ
רִ
י
ם

מַפָּה   פָּנוּי   שָׁנַיִם   הַגָּן   גִּיר

הָמוּם   יָדַיִם   רַבִּין   הָמָן   אָדָם

רוּת and דָּן were excited to get lots of candy in their
Misloach Manot basket. However, all the candies got
mixed up. Arrange the letters on the candies to spell some
Hebrew words you already know. Use each letter once.

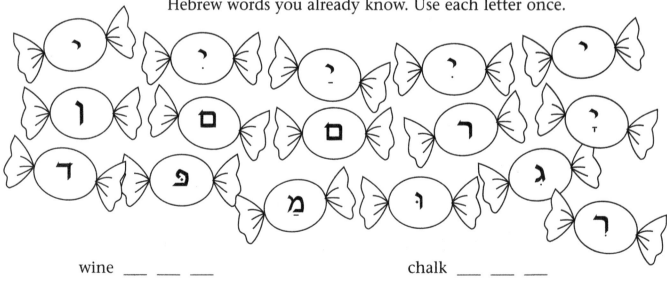

wine __ __ __   chalk __ __ __

hand __ __   water __ __ __

Purim __ __ __ __ __

19

Lesson 7

KEY WORD:
פּוּרִים

HELP YOUR דָּג SWIM

Play this game with one or two friends. Each one picks a stream to swim and reads the words it contains. Your turn is over when you make a mistake, and you must start over at the beginning on your next turn. The first one to swim all the way to the big pool is the winner.

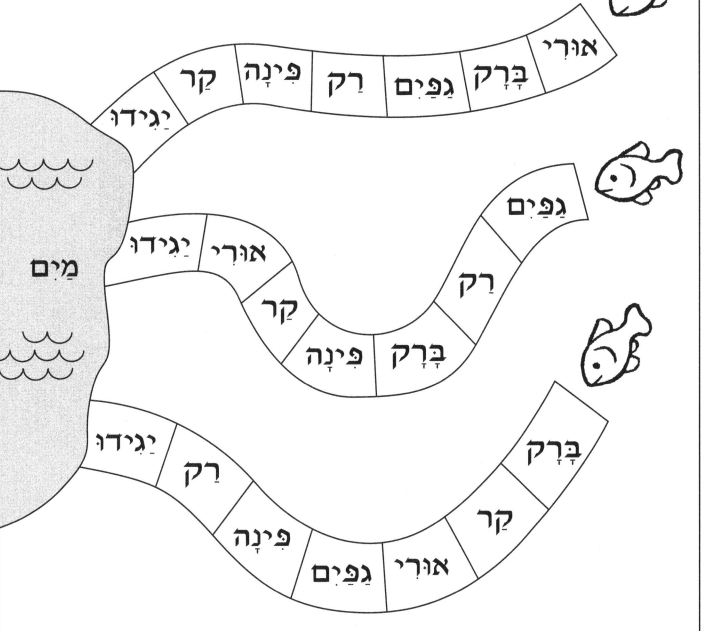

KEY WORD:

חַלָּה

LETTER HINT

The ת and the ט make the same sound. They look like
two legs and each one has a big **t**oe sticking out.

Color the **t**oes in the ת and ט below.
Color the ה in a different color. Notice it does **not**
have a toe sticking out.

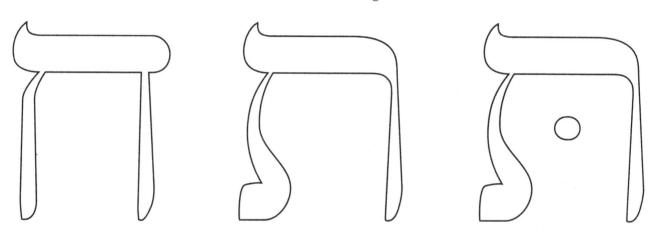

Read the words below. Remember the hints!

אַתָּה	תָּמָר	תִּמִי	א. מַתַּי
חָתוּל	רוּתִי	חוּפָּה	ב. תְּמוּר
חֲתִימָה	תַּחַת	חֲתוּנָה	ג. רַחֲמִים

Now, circle every letter that makes a "T" sound using the
color you used to color the toes in the ת and ט. Then
circle every ה in the color you used above for that letter.

Lesson 8
KEY WORD:
חַלָּה

PLAY DARTS WITH A FRIEND

Take turns reading any word on the dart board. When you read a word correctly, you score the number of points written in that space. Read each word only once. When all the words have been read, total your scores.

1 אָח	1 שָׁת
2 לָתַת	2 חָלָק
1 חַג	1 פֶּה
2 מַתָּן	4 חֲתִימָה
4 תִּקּוּן	2 אָמַר
3 אִלּוּם	3 חֲגִיגָה
5 חֲמִשִּׁיָּה	
4 חֲתוּנָה	3 חָלוֹם
2 חָמָל	2 חַיִל
1 חָל	3 חִלּוּק
4 חִצּוּי	1 תָּם
2 חוֹם	2 חָלָא
1 חָת	1 חָם

												Total
Player 1:												
Player 2:												

22

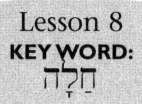

WEDDING VIDEO

Look at page 60 of your Workbook. These are pictures from the חֲתֻנָה of אָרִיק and חַנָה. You were there to make the video. Draw the video scenes here. Use the words in the dictionary below in your captions.

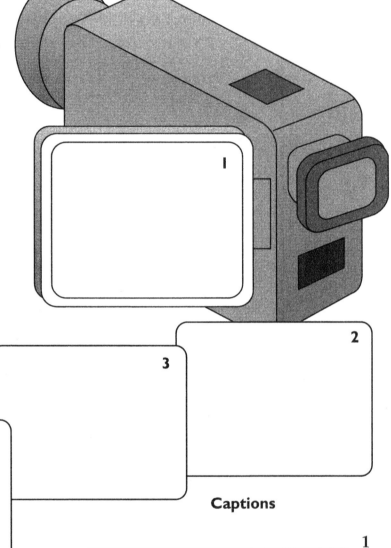

Dictionary	
wedding canopy	חוּפָּה
cat (male)	חָתוּל
cat (female)	חֲתוּלָה
wedding	חֲתֻנָה
Rabbi	רַבִּי
under	תַּחַת

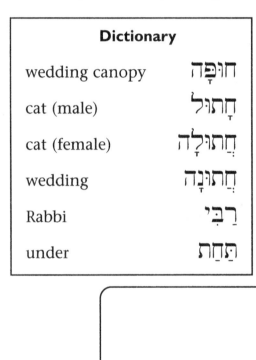

Captions

1 _____

2 _____

3 _____

4 _____

5 _____

6 _____

SILLY SENTENCES

Some of the sentences below describe silly or
impossible situations. Read all the sentences and
circle the silly ones. Here is an English example:

Dad is in the house.   *(Mom is in the fish.)*   **The hand is in the water.**

1.   הַדָג בַּמַיִם.

2.   אִמָא בַּדָג.

3.   מַצָה תַּחַת הַהַגָדָה.

4.   אַתָה אַבָא.

5.   הַיַיִן תַּחַת הַבַּיִת.

6.   חַלָה בַּבַּיִת.

7.   הַבַּיִת תַּחַת הַמַיִם.

8.   הַגִיר בַּיָד.

Now, draw a picture of your favorite sentence.

Lesson 9
KEY WORDS:
מִצְוָה הַבְדָלָה

SPICE UP YOUR READING!

Each section of the הַבְדָלָה spice box below contains one word written three different ways. Share the reading with your partner. First, one of you reads the first half of the word and the other finishes the word. Then switch parts.

מַר גִּישׁ	לֵב לוּב	מִק דָשׁ
מַרְגִּישׁ	לְבלוּב	מְקַדֵּשׁ
מַרְגִּישׁ	לְבְלוּב	מְקַדֵּשׁ
מַב דִּיל	וֹל נָה	תַּב לִין
מַבְדִּיל	וְלָנָה	תַּבְלִין
מַבְדִּיל	וְלָנָה	תַּבְלִין
פָּת חָה	תֵּק וָה	דְּק דּוּק
פְּתָחָה	תִּקְוָה	דְּקְדּוּק
פְּתָחָה	תִּקְוָה	דְּקְדּוּק

Lesson 9

CUT-UP WORDS

The words on the right have been "cut" into two pieces.
On the left side, the words have been put back together.
First read each cut word, then read each whole word.

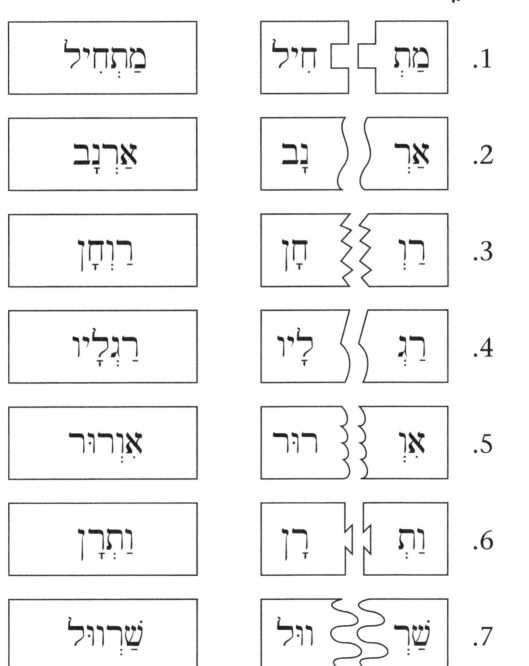

מַתְחִיל	מַתְ חִיל	1.
אַרְנָב	אַר נָב	2.
רוּחָן	רוּ חָן	3.
רַגְלָיו	רַגְ לָיו	4.
אוֹרוּר	אוֹ רוּר	5.
וַתֵּרֶן	וַתֵּ רֶן	6.
שַׁרְווּל	שַׁרְ ווּל	7.

26

Lesson 9

KEY WORDS:
מִצְוָה   הַבְדָלָה

SLIDING WORDS

Cut out Strip 1 and Strip 3. Cut along dotted lines on Strip 2.
Insert Strips 1 and 3 in the slits so that the Hebrew shows through.
Move either strip to form different words. How many combinations
can you read in a minute? (There are 36 possible combinations.)

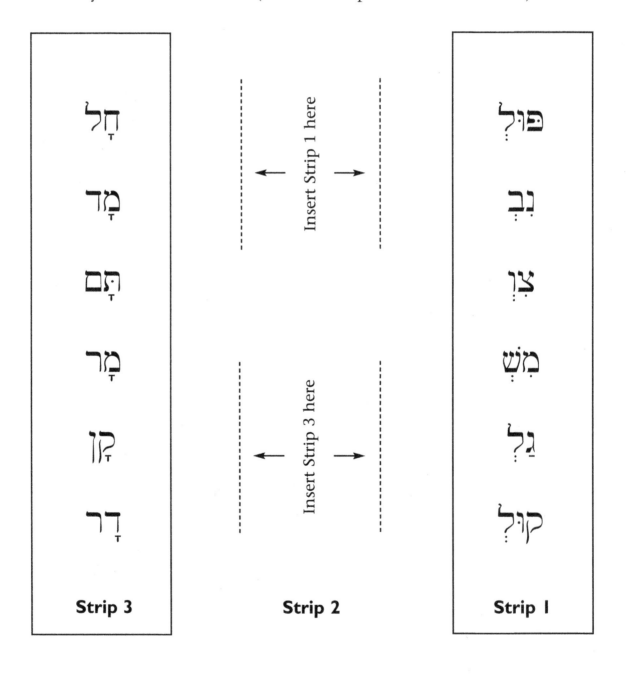

	Strip 2	
Strip 3		Strip 1

Insert Strip 1 here

Insert Strip 3 here

Strip 3   **Strip 2**   **Strip 1**

PURIM COSTUMES

Read the following story.
Then write the children's names under their pictures.

פּוּרִים. הַמִּשְׁפָּחָה בַּבַּיִת.

אַבָּא: מִי אַתְּ?

רִבְקָה: אֲנִי חֲתוּלָה.

אִמָּא: מִי אַתָּה?

דָּוִד: אֲנִי הָמָן

Circle the Hebrew sentence that matches the picture above it.

מִי אַתָּה?	אֲנִי אִמָּא.	אֲנִי בַּבַּיִת.
מִי הָמָן?	מִי אַתְּ?	מִי בַּבַּיִת?
אֲנִי חֲתוּלָה.	מִי בַּבַּיִת?	הַמִּשְׁפָּחָה בַּבַּיִת.

Write the Hebrew word.

New Vocabulary

כַּדוּר

PLAY BALL!

Read the words below each basket. Then draw a basketball in the correct place.

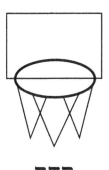  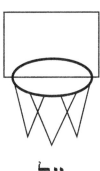 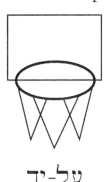

תַּחַת	בַּ/בְּ	עַל	עַל-יַד

CREATE A CARTOON

Illustrate this comic strip. It tells the story of a חָתוּל (cat) chasing a כַּדוּר (ball) through the house and into the fishbowl. Make sure you understand each sentence. Share your masterpiece with your friends.

3. דָג בַּמַיִם. כַּדוּר עַל-יַד דָג. חָתוּל עַל-יַד דָג.	2. כַּדוּר עַל-יַד אִמָא. חָתוּל עַל-יַד אִמָא.	1. חָתוּל בַּבַיִת. כַּדוּר בַּבַיִת.

6. כַּדוּר עַל-יַד חָתוּל.	5. דָג בָּחָתוּל.	4. דָג תַּחַת חָתוּל.

PUZZLE OUT THE SECRET WORDS

Complete the puzzles in Hebrew. Do not use vowels.
Write the letters from the shaded boxes on the lines below.

1. In the class

2. Hebrew

3. Family

4. Passover "bread"

5. A commandment

6. You (m.)

‗ __ __ ‗ __ ‗
  ָ   :   .   __

Draw a picture to illustrate this word.

1. What

2. Blessing over wine

3. Holiday before Pesach

4. Shabbat bread

5. Class

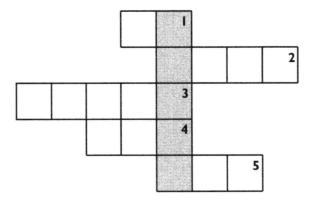

‗ __ __ __ __
  ָ   ָ   :   .

Draw a picture to illustrate this word.

Lesson 10

KEY WORDS:

עִבְרִית כִּתָּה

SPEED READING

By now you can read many Hebrew words. Are you reading
as fast as you would like? To read faster, try this:

1. Have a friend time you as you read.
2. Read as many words below as you can in one minute.
3. If you make a mistake, your friend should say, "Try again."
   Then you must read the word again.
4. Write down how many words you read correctly.
5. Read the words again. See if you can beat your old score.

1. עַל אָב כּוּר קַו שׁוּב

2. כִּפָּה עוּגָה כִּתָּה אֲבָל עָלוּב

3. עִבְרִית שָׁבוּעַ כַּדוּר עָלֶיהָ בְּכִתָּה

4. אֲוִיר עֲמִידָה הַבְדָלָה עַכָּבִישׁ חַקְיָן

5. עֲבַרְיָן כַּוַּנְתִּי יִשְׁתַּבַּח עַתִּיקָה מִצְבָּעָה

Words I Can Read in a Minute

	1st Try	2nd Try	3rd Try
My scores:			

32

Lesson 11
KEY WORDS:

פֶּסַח יִשְׂרָאֵל

VOWEL HINTS

The new vowels ▇ and ▇ look like little eggs.
Three **eggs** or five **eggs**, they both make the sound of "**eh**" as in "**eggs**."

Color in yellow the vowels that make the "**eh**" sound in the eggs below.

1. Color in yellow all the "**eh**" vowels in the words below.
2. Color in aqua (blue-green) all the "**ah**" vowels in the words below.
3. Read the vowel sounds to your teacher or partner.
4. Then, read the words.

1. דֶּגֶל   הֶאֱמִין   כֶּלֶב   אֱמֶת   כֶּבֶשׂ
2. פֶּרַח   אֶחָד   קֶבַע   שְׁמָא   קֶמַח
3. שָׁוֶה   נָוֶה   עָשָׂה   כַּלֶּבֶת   אֲדֶמֶת

SMILES AND MARSHMALLOWS

The ס has a big smile at the bottom. The ם looks like a
marshmallow, and comes only at the end of a word. Decorate
the ס and the ם so they look like a smile and a marshmallow.

מַיִם   סֵדֶר

Read the words containing ס and ם.

שָׁמַיִם   סְכוּם   נִמְאַס   פִּנְקָס   שַׁחֲקָנִים
סִדּוּר   קְיָם   פַּרְנֵס   סַמּוּם   בִּסְפּוּס

KEY WORDS:
פֶּסַח יִשְׂרָאֵל

MYSTERY PICTURE

It is customary to invite guests on פֶּסַח to share our סֵדֶר with us. When dessert is over, one special guest comes to every סֵדֶר for an "after dinner drink." Find the Hebrew name of our honored guest in the picture below.

Color blue all the spaces with words that have the **S** sound in them.
Color yellow all the spaces with words that have the **V** sound in them.
Color black all the spaces with words that have the **B** sound in them.
Color brown all the spaces with words that have the **SH** sound in them.
Leave white all the spaces that do not have words with these sounds in them.

צָבָא		וֶרֶד	
שֵׁם	שָׁקֵד		מִצְוָה
אָב	רַבָּה	בָּא	שַׂעַר
אֵשׁ	קִבְּלוּ	קִשְׁקוּשׁ	דָוִד
צַב	אֵלִיָהוּ הַנָבִיא	קָדוֹשׁ	אֶבֶן
שָׂר	בְּמְהֵרָה	בִּרְכַּת	
שָׁם	בַּיָמִים	בּוּל	פָּגַשְׁתִּי	עִבְרִית
לֵוִי	בָּה	בִּלְבּוּל	כָּשֵׁר	דֶבֶק
נִסִּים	נָשִׂיא	שָׂעִיר	נִימוּס	סַנְהֶדְרִין
שַׂר	הַשָׂדֶה	שִׂיחָה	פַּרְנָס	שִׂמְחָה

The Hebrew name of our special guest is _____ _____.

Lesson 11

FLY TO יִשְׂרָאֵל

Play this game with one, two, or three friends. Each picks a starting country. Take turns reading and translating the words on your path to Israel. If you make a mistake, your turn is over and you must return to your country. The first to arrive in יִשְׂרָאֵל is the winner.

RUSSIA

| יֶלֶד | מָגֵן דָוִד | יַלְדָה | דֶּגֶל | מַחְבֶּרֶת | עַל־יַד | בְּכִתָּה | עִבְרִית |

U.S.A.

| דֶּגֶל | עַל־יַד | מַחְבֶּרֶת | יֶלֶד | בְּכִתָּה | מָגֵן דָוִד | יַלְדָה | עִבְרִית |

ETHIOPIA

| בְּכִתָּה | מַחְבֶּרֶת | יַלְדָה | עַל־יַד | יֶלֶד | מָגֵן דָוִד | דֶּגֶל | עִבְרִית |

ARGENTINA

| מַחְבֶּרֶת | יַלְדָה | עַל־יַד | מָגֵן דָוִד | דֶּגֶל | בְּכִתָּה | יֶלֶד | עִבְרִית |

יִשְׂרָאֵל

KEY WORDS:
אֶלֶף סֵפֶר

THE STORY OF פַּ, פָ, AND ף

Once there was a mother who had three children:

Pay   פַּ

Fay   פָ

Final Fay   ף

How could she tell them apart? Every morning she **p**ut a dot inside פַּ. She always **f**orgot to put the dot in פָ, and ף was so **f**unny that it **f**ell down laughing at the end of every word. Read these words containing all three children:

אַלְפַּיִם   אֶלֶף   רָפִי   סִפּוּר   סֵפֶר   שָׂפָה

צָפוֹן   פַּרְפַּר   כַּף   פֶּסַח   קָפֶה   צָעִיף

PICTURE THIS

Read the sentences in this story. Make sure you understand each sentence.
Complete the picture that the story describes.

פֶּסַח בַּבַּיִת.

כֶּלֶב בַּבַּיִת.

חָתוּל בַּבַּיִת.

חַלָה לֹא בַּבַּיִת.

כֶּלֶב עַל-יַד חָתוּל.

מַצָה תַּחַת הַגָדָה.

עִבְרִית עַל הַגָדָה.

Lesson 12
KEY WORDS:
סֵפֶר אָלֶף

MAKE A LITTLE סֵפֶר

1. Take a plain piece of paper.
   Fold it into four even pieces.
   Cut on the folds so you have
   four little pieces of paper.

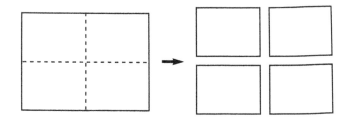

2. Fold each piece in half.
   Put all the pieces together
   so that they form book pages.

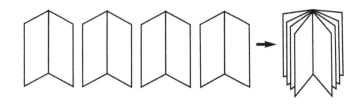

3. Staple the pages together at the
   fold or punch two holes and
   tie the book together with
   a ribbon.

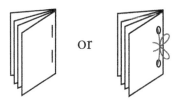

   or

4. Hold your סֵפֶר so that it opens in the direction of עִבְרִית.
   Write on the cover:

   הַסֵפֶר שֶׁל _____

   That means it's your book, so write in your name.

5. Now, write in עִבְרִית and illustrate some sentences or a story.
   See the sentences on page 18 of your זְמַן לִקְרֹא Volume Two
   workbook for ideas. Use the Dictionary on pages 86 and 87 for help.
   Here are some other words you might want to use:

ball	כַּדוּר	**I have**	יֵשׁ לִי	**door**	דֶלֶת
champion	אַלוּף	**money**	כֶּסֶף	**basketball**	כַּדוּר-סַל

6. Add more pages to your book if you wish.
   Share your book with your classmates.

Lesson 13
KEY WORDS:
שָׁלוֹם בֹּקֶר טוֹב

VOWEL HINT

When you look at the וֹ vowel, think of a little boy or girl playing ball. The ball has been thrown <u>o</u>ver the child's head so that the vowel reminds you of the sound "o" for <u>o</u>ver. Finish the picture below so that it looks like a child playing ball. Be creative!

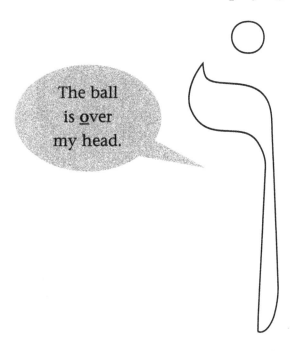

The ball is <u>o</u>ver my head.

Read the words below.

1.	אָמַר	אוֹמֵר	אוֹמֶרֶת	אוֹמְרִים אוֹמְרוֹת
2.	עוֹלָם	אָבוֹת	קָדוֹשׁ	עוֹשֶׂה שָׁלוֹם
3.	שׁוֹפָר	עוֹמֵד	לוֹמֵד	שִׁיפּוֹן שָׁעוֹן
4.	רָצָה	רוֹצֶה	רוֹצָה	רוֹצִים רוֹצוֹת

38

KEY WORDS:

שָׁלוֹם בֹּקֶר טוֹב

OVER AND OVER AGAIN

The vowel ⬛ is just a short way of writing the וֹ vowel.
What sound do both vowels make? _____ The ⬛ vowel
also reminds us of a ball going <u>o</u>ver someone's head.

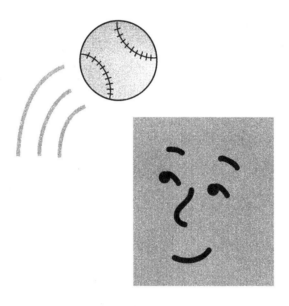

With a yellow marker or crayon, color the vowels in the four lines
below that make the sound of "o" as in "<u>o</u>ver." Then read the lines.
Watch out for the וֹ vowel. Remember, it has a different sound.

1. קָדוֹשׁ בֹּקֶר קָדוֹשׁ טוֹב לֹא

2. גָּדוֹל הָוָה בוֹא סוּסָה פֹּה

3. פִּתְאֹם הַיוֹם לִצְעֹד טוֹבָה דוֹד

4. צָהֹב אָפֹר כִּפּוֹר הוֹסִיפוּ חֲנוּיוֹת

KEY WORDS:

שָׁלוֹם בֹּקֶר טוֹב

LETTER HINT

The letter ט is open at the <u>t</u>op. What sound does this letter make? _____
The letter מ looks like <u>M</u>oses on the <u>M</u>ountain. It makes the sound of _____

Draw an arrow pointing to the opening in the top of the ט.
Color the מ to look like <u>M</u>oses on the <u>M</u>ountain.

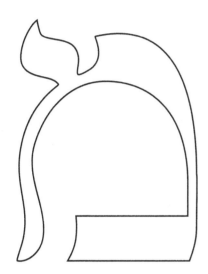 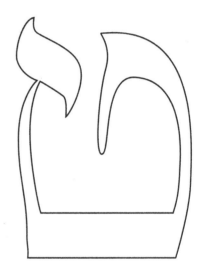

Read the words below. Remember the hints for the letters ט and מ!
If it helps you, color the letters that are difficult.

טְטָפוֹת	מֶמְשָׁלָה	טוֹעָה	טָרֶף	מִמוּל
לוֹמֶדֶת	טוֹבָה	מוֹרָה	מוֹרֶה	טִפֵּל
טוֹרְדָן	טִפֵּר	שוֹמֵר	טֶנֶא	טָמִיר
פְּעָמִים	טַחֲנָה	טוֹפֵחַ	תַמְחוּי	מַחֲנֶה

Lesson 13

KEY WORDS:

שָׁלוֹם בֹּקֶר טוֹב

STORY TIME

Read the story below.

אֲנִי בַּכִּתָּה. אֲנִי יַלְדָּה. אֲנִי לוֹמֶדֶת.

הַמּוֹרָה לֹא בַּכִּתָּה. הַיֶּלֶד יוֹסִי בַּכִּתָּה.

יוֹסִי לֹא לוֹמֵד. יוֹסִי תַּחַת הַסֵּפֶר.

Answer these questions about the story with כֵּן or לֹא.

1. יוֹסִי מוֹרֶה? _____

2. הַיַּלְדָּה לוֹמֶדֶת? _____

3. יוֹסִי בַּכִּתָּה? _____

4. הַכֶּלֶב בַּכִּתָּה? _____

5. יוֹסִי תַּחַת הַסֵּפֶר? _____

In the picture below, cross out anything that does not belong.

41

Lesson 14

YOUR FAVORITE MEAL

Check the sentences that describe what you like to eat or drink.
Then draw a picture below of the foods you checked.

Girls' List מָה אַתְּ אוֹהֶבֶת?	**Boys' List** מָה אַתָּה אוֹהֵב?
אֲנִי אוֹהֶבֶת שׁוֹקוֹלָד. ❑	אֲנִי אוֹהֵב שׁוֹקוֹלָד. ❑
אֲנִי אוֹהֶבֶת קָפֶה. ❑	אֲנִי אוֹהֵב קָפֶה. ❑
אֲנִי אוֹהֶבֶת פִּיצָה. ❑	אֲנִי אוֹהֵב פִּיצָה. ❑
אֲנִי אוֹהֶבֶת דָג עִם לִימוֹן. ❑	אֲנִי אוֹהֵב דָג עִם לִימוֹן. ❑
אֲנִי אוֹהֶבֶת חַלָה. ❑	אֲנִי אוֹהֵב חַלָה. ❑
אֲנִי אוֹהֶבֶת קוֹקָה קוֹלָה. ❑	אֲנִי אוֹהֵב קוֹקָה קוֹלָה. ❑
אֲנִי אוֹהֶבֶת סְפָּגֶטִי. ❑	אֲנִי אוֹהֵב סְפָּגֶטִי. ❑
אֲנִי אוֹהֶבֶת לִימוֹנָדָה. ❑	אֲנִי אוֹהֵב לִימוֹנָדָה. ❑
אֲנִי אוֹהֶבֶת מַצָה. ❑	אֲנִי אוֹהֵב מַצָה. ❑
אֲנִי אוֹהֶבֶת מַיִם. ❑	אֲנִי אוֹהֵב מַיִם. ❑
אֲנִי אוֹהֶבֶת הַמְבּוּרְגֶר עִם קֶטְשׁוֹפּ. ❑	אֲנִי אוֹהֵב הַמְבּוּרְגֶר עִם קֶטְשׁוֹפּ. ❑

Lesson 14

KEY WORDS:

סְלִיחָה   בְּבַקָשָׁה

WHAT'S YOUR NUMBER?

Practice reading the Hebrew words for the numbers from 0 to 9.
Read them as quickly as you can.

In the spaces below, write your phone number in Hebrew words.

_____ _____ _____ _____ _____ _____ _____

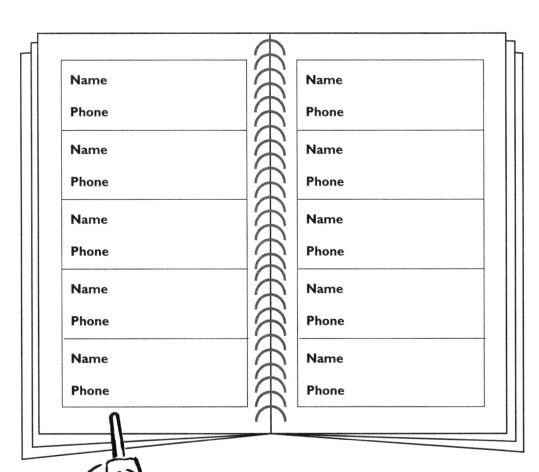

0 =	אֶפֶס
1 =	אַחַת
2 =	שְׁתַּיִם
3 =	שָׁלוֹשׁ
4 =	אַרְבַּע
5 =	חָמֵשׁ
6 =	שֵׁשׁ
7 =	שֶׁבַע
8 =	שְׁמוֹנֶה
9 =	תֵּשַׁע

In Hebrew, number digits are written from left to right, just
like in English! Make a Hebrew phone directory. Take turns
sharing your phone number in Hebrew with your friends.
Write down each other's numbers as they are read. Check
each other's work to see if it was done correctly.

Lesson 15
KEY WORD:
מַזָּל טוֹב

READING PAGE

1. זֶה   זֹאת   זֶהוּ   זוּג   זוּז

2. זִיו   זֶפֶת   זֶרַע   זָנָב   זֶבַח

3. תַּמוּז   אֶרֶז   תַּפּוּז   זִמְזוּם   מוּזְמָן

4. זָהָב   צָהֹב   אָזֵן   צֹאן   מָזוֹן

5. זֶהוּת   זוֹעֵף   שׁוֹטֵף   הִזְדַמְנוּת   הִשְׁתַּכְּרוּת

6. מוּזָר   נֶעֱזָר   מִזְרָח   הֶחֱזִיר   הַמַּחֲזִיר

7. זֶמֶר   זַמֶרֶת   זַמָּרִים   זִמְרִיָה   תִזְמֹרֶת

Cool Hebrew Phrases

הָעוֹלָם הַזֶה דוֹמֶה לִפְרוֹזְדוֹר בִּפְנֵי הָעוֹלָם הַבָּא:

"This world is like a waiting room for the world to come."

— Rabbi Jacob, *Pirke Avot* 4: 21

Lesson 15

KEY WORDS:

מַזָּל טוֹב   חַג שָׂמֵחַ   בֵּית-כְּנֶסֶת

VOWEL HUNT

Read all the words in the pot of chicken soup below.
Draw a מַצָּה ball around each word that has the **ay** sound in it.
Delicious!

בֵּין

בְּלִי

יָבֵשׁ   אֲבוֹתֵינוּ   דָּנִיאֵל

אֲנִי

יוֹצֵר

חַיֵּינוּ   יְסַד

אַשְׁרֵי

אַיָל   לִפְנֵי   שֵׁם

עָלֵינוּ

נִצֵּיד   בְּנֵי   עֵיפוֹת   אֵיתָן

אֵין

עָיֵף   שֶׁהֶחֱיָנוּ

Lesson 15

KEY WORDS:

מַזָּל טוֹב   חַג שָׂמֵחַ   בֵּית-כְּנֶסֶת

WHAT DO YOU SAY?

Imagine you are visiting יִשְׂרָאֵל. What would you say in עִבְרִית in each of the following situations? For each sentence, use one of the six choices at the bottom of the page. Write the correct choice on each line.

1. It's פֶּסַח. You see your friends in synagogue.

   _____

2. You accidentally bump into someone.

   _____

3. You politely ask for another piece of cake.

   _____

4. You greet your aunt at seven in the morning.

   _____

5. Your cousin celebrates his בַּר-מִצְוָה in Jerusalem.

   _____

6. You say good-bye to everyone before you fly home.

   _____

בְּבַקָּשָׁה	בֹּקֶר טוֹב	סְלִיחָה
חַג שָׂמֵחַ	מַזָּל טוֹב	שָׁלוֹם

46

Lesson 15

בֵּית-כְּנֶסֶת   חַג שָׂמֵחַ   מַזָל טוֹב

FOUR IN A ROW

Play this game with a partner. One player is "X", the other is
"O". Take turns reading one Hebrew word below. If you read the
word correctly, mark that box with your X or O. The first to get
four words in a straight line in any direction is the winner.

כּוּוֹן	זֹאת	גָדוֹל	בָּטוּחַ	אֹזֶן	יָרֵחַ
לוּחַ	זוֹנֵחַ	מִתְפַּתֵּחַ	עֶפְרוֹן	סוֹלֵחַ	כִּסֵא
תִזְמֹרֶת	אוֹרֵחַ	זֶה	זְמְרִיָה	חַג	לוֹעֲזִי
צוֹרֵחַ	חָזוֹן	שָׂמֵחַ	מָזוֹן	מִתְקַלֵחַ	מָטוֹס
קָטָן	עֵט	זַעֲטוּט	תַּפּוּחַ	רוּחַ	כֵּיוָן
כַּסֶפֶת	מָתוּחַ	כִּסְלֵו	מַטָּה	לוֹעֵז	חֲבֵרִים

47

Lesson 15

KEY WORDS:

מַזָּל טוֹב חַג שָׂמֵחַ בֵּית-כְּנֶסֶת

CRACK THE CODE!

Did you know that every Hebrew letter also has a number value?
Look at the number value for each letter.

א	ב/בּ	ג	ד	ה	ו	ז	ח	ט	י	כ/ךּ
1	2	3	4	5	6	7	8	9	10	20

ל	מ/ם	נ/ן	ס	ע	פ/פּ/ף	צ	ק	ר	שׁ/שׂ	ת
30	40	50	60	70	80	90	100	200	300	400

Write the Hebrew letter for each number on the lines below. Use final letters at the end of words. Match each Hebrew sentence to its picture.

8 6 30 5   4 10   30 70   50 9 100   200 10 3

1 40 1   8 40 300   3 8

10 50 4   2 6 9   30 7 40

1 60 20 5   30 70   30 6 4 3   50 6 200 80 70

48

Lesson 16

BE A DETECTIVE

The "VO" sound always tries to hide in Hebrew. It is hiding in 11 of the words below. Your job is to discover all its hiding places. Color all the "O" sounds in yellow. Color all the "V" sounds in blue. Color all the "VO" sounds in green. Then fill in the blanks to describe the clues that helped you find these sounds.

1. צַוָּה   מִצְוָה   מִצְוֹת   מַצּוֹת   מִצְוֹת

2. וּמִצְוֹת   הַמִּצְוָה   הַמִּצְוֹת   בְּמִצְוֹת   בְּמִצְוֹתָיו

3. עָוֹן   עוֹנָה   וְעָוֹן   עוֹנוֹת   עֲוֹנוֹת

4. עֲוֹנֵנוּ   עֲוֹנוֹתֵינוּ   עוֹיֵן   עֵדוֹת   עֲוֹנָתִיוֹת

1. A ו makes a "V" sound whenever it is followed by a _____.

2. A ו makes an "O" sound whenever it follows a _____.

3. A ו makes a "VO" sound whenever it follows a _____ or a _____.

49

LOTS OF DOTS

Play this game with a friend. Turn to page 50 in Volume Two of your זְמַן לִקְרֹא Workbook. When you read a word correctly, draw a line connecting two dots like this ●—● or this ❗ (not like this ✎). If the line you draw completes a small square, write your initials in the square (like this: HZ). Continue reading until all the lines are drawn. The one with the most squares is the winner.

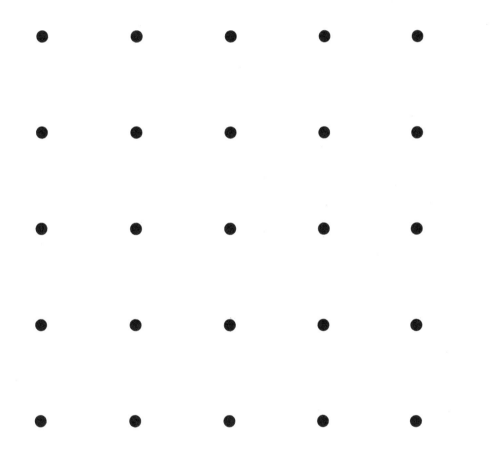

You can play this game using any Reading Page in your זְמַן לִקְרֹא Workbook. Copy the dots onto a sheet of paper and play the game any time you need to review your reading. Or, you can draw the dots on the chalkboard and play as two teams.

Lesson 16

עֵץ חַיִּים מִצְוֺת

מִי אַתָּה? מִי אַתְּ?

Write a story about yourself. Some words you may need are in the box below. Or, use the Dictionary on pages 86 and 87 of your זְמַן לִקְרֹא Workbook Volume Two. Here are some questions to answer in your story:

Girls	Boys
מִי אַתְּ?	מִי אַתָּה?
מָה אַתְּ אוֹהֶבֶת?	מָה אַתָּה אוֹהֵב?
אֵיפֹה אַתְּ לוֹמֶדֶת?	אֵיפֹה אַתָּה לוֹמֵד?
מָה אַתְּ לוֹמֶדֶת?	מָה אַתָּה לוֹמֵד?

_____

_____

_____

_____

_____

_____

_____

Dictionary מִלוֹן

at school	בְּבֵית-סֵפֶר	I	אֲנִי
Hebrew	עִבְרִית	boy	יֶלֶד
family	מִשְׁפָּחָה	girl	יַלְדָּה

51

Lesson 17

KEY WORDS:

בְּרָכָה שֻׁלְחָן

OO – ANOTHER VOWEL HINT!

The new vowel looks like a train going downhill.
At the end of the train you find the cab**oo**se.

Go down the hill by reading each word correctly.

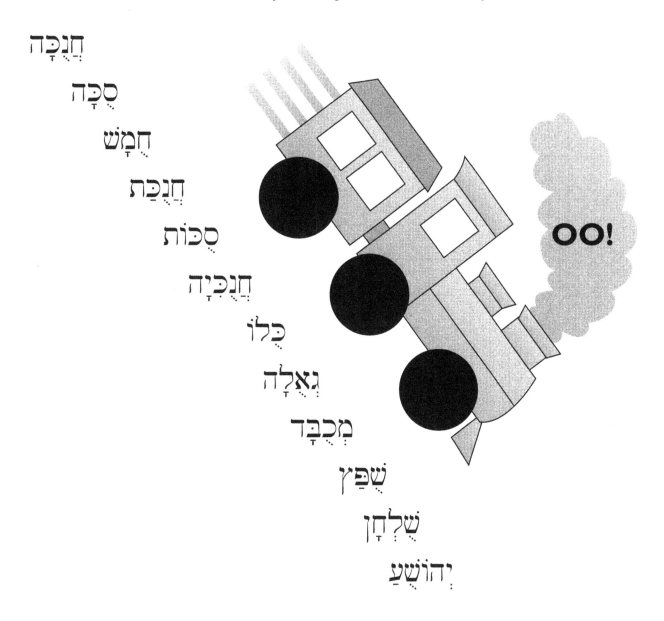

חֲנֻכָּה

סֻכָּה

חֻמָשׁ

חֲנֻכַּת

סֻכּוֹת

חֲנֻכִּיָה

כֻּלוֹ

גָּאֻלָה

מְכֻבָּד

שֻׁפַּץ

שֻׁלְחָן

יְהוֹשֻׁעַ

OO!

52

Lesson 17

בְּרָכָה שֻׁלְחָן

CRACK THE CODE!

To solve the riddle, cross out all the words that contain a "CH" sound as in Chanukah.

בֵּרַכְנוּ	בָּרְכוּ	בְּרָכוֹת	בְּרוּכִים	בְּרָכָה
חֲנִיכוֹת	חֲנוּכִי	חֲנֻכִּיָּה	חֲנֻכַּת	חֲנֻכָּה
רַחֲמִים	חִדּוּשׁ	קָדוֹשׁ	חֶסֶד	חֵן
אוֹכְלוֹת	אוֹכְלִים	אוֹכֶלֶת	אוֹכֵל	לֶאֱכֹל
בַּשִׂיחָה	בַּסֻּכָּה	סֻכָּה	סֻכָּה	סוֹכְנוּת

"What בְּרָכָה do you make around a שֻׁלְחָן that is not in your בַּיִת?"

_____ _____

Draw a picture to illustrate the answer you found.

Lesson 17

KEY WORDS:

בְּרָכָה שֻׁלְחָן

שַׁבָּת שָׁלוֹם

Read this story about שַׁבָּת. Underline all the words about people.
Circle all the words that are places. Draw a box around the food words.

Example: הַיַּלְדָּה עִם הַמַּצָּה בַּבַּיִת.

שַׁבָּת בַּבֹּקֶר.

שַׁבָּת שָׁלוֹם.

שַׁבָּת בַּבַּיִת.

חַלָּה וְיַיִן עַל הַשֻּׁלְחָן.

הַמִּשְׁפָּחָה לֹא עַל-יַד הַשֻּׁלְחָן.

הַמִּשְׁפָּחָה לֹא בַּבַּיִת.

אֵיפֹה הַמִּשְׁפָּחָה?

בְּבֵית-הַכְּנֶסֶת.

Choose the correct answer for each of the following questions:

מַצָּה וְהַגָּדָה יַיִן וְחַלָּה יֶלֶד וְיַלְדָּה	1. מָה עַל הַשֻּׁלְחָן?
עֵץ חַיִּים בְּרָכָה הַמִּשְׁפָּחָה	2. מִי בְּבֵית-הַכְּנֶסֶת?

Lesson 17
KEY WORDS:
בְּרָכָה שֻׁלְחָן

IT'S BIRTHDAY TIME!

יוֹם הֻלֶּדֶת is the Hebrew phrase for birthday.
What do you think יוֹם הֻלֶּדֶת שָׂמֵחַ means?

_____   _____

There are many Hebrew birthday songs. The simplest is sung to the tune of "Happy Birthday To You." Repeat this line four times:

יוֹם הֻלֶּדֶת שָׂמֵחַ

Here is another favorite. Fill in the person's name on the blank line.
Sing the first version for a boy, and the second version for a girl.
Read the words for both versions of this song.

for a girl	for a boy
הַיּוֹם יוֹם הֻלֶּדֶת (3 times)	הַיּוֹם יוֹם הֻלֶּדֶת (3 times)
לְ_____ •	לְ_____ •
חַג לָהּ שָׂמֵחַ	חַג לוֹ שָׂמֵחַ
וְזֵר לָהּ פּוֹרֵחַ	וְזֵר לוֹ פּוֹרֵחַ
הַיּוֹם יוֹם הֻלֶּדֶת	הַיּוֹם יוֹם הֻלֶּדֶת
לְ_____ •	לְ_____ •

KEY WORDS:

בְּרָכָה שֻׁלְחָן

CHARADES

Play this game with one or more friends.
You will need to have the following objects:

סֵפֶר, שֻׁלְחָן, כִּסֵּא, מַחְבֶּרֶת, גִּיר, עִפָּרוֹן

Choose one of the boxes below. Arrange the objects according to the instructions written in the box. The other players must guess which box you have chosen. Whoever guesses correctly gets to take the next turn.

הָעִפָּרוֹן תַּחַת הַסֵּפֶר.	הָעִפָּרוֹן בַּמַחְבֶּרֶת.
הַסֵּפֶר עַל-יַד הָעִפָּרוֹן.	הַסֵּפֶר עַל-יַד הַמַחְבֶּרֶת.
הָעִפָּרוֹן וְהַסֵּפֶר עַל הַכִּסֵּא.	הַגִּיר עַל-יַד הָעִפָּרוֹן.
הָעִפָּרוֹן תַּחַת הַכִּסֵּא.	הַגִּיר תַּחַת הַשֻּׁלְחָן.
הַמַחְבֶּרֶת בַּסֵּפֶר.	הָעִפָּרוֹן עַל הַכִּסֵּא.
הַכִּסֵּא עַל-יַד הַשֻּׁלְחָן.	הַגִּיר וְהָעִפָּרוֹן בַּסֵּפֶר.

הַגִּיר תַּחַת הַכִּסֵּא.

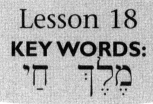
BE A COMPUTER WHIZ

Fill in the computer screen with the Hebrew letters in alphabetical
order. Look at the letters in the box on page 48 if you need help.
Write each final letter in the same box as its regular form.

57

Lesson 18

מֶלֶךְ חַי

חַי, חַי, וְקַיָם

Read each word on the חַי necklace.
Color in each space after you read the word correctly.

טוּרִי פָּנַי סִינַי מֶלֶךְ

חֲשְׁמוֹנַאי שְׂפָתַי טִפּוֹתַי רַבּוֹתַי

אִמּוֹתַי בָּרוּךְ אֲבוֹתַי לָךְ

דְּבָרַי יַלְדֵי לָךְ שִׁירֵי

כִּיסֵי זְמָנַי

מוֹעֲדַי שֶׁלָּךְ

שֶׁלָּךְ מְשַׂגֵּי

עָלַי לְהַחֲיוֹת

אָזַי

דַּי

גְּבוּרוֹתַי אֱמוּנֵי

58

Lesson 18
KEY WORDS:
מֶלֶךְ חַי

SPEED READING

The list of words below is in אָלֶף-בֵּית order.
How quickly can you read them?

1. Have a friend time you as you read.

2. Going down each column, read as many words as you can in one minute.

3. If you make a mistake, your friend should say, "Try again." Then you must start again from the beginning.

4. Write down how long it took you to read the words correctly.

5. Read the words again. See if you can beat your old score.

19. קָפֶה	10. יִשְׂרָאֵל	1. אוֹרֵחַ
20. רַךְ	11. כַּוֶּנֶת	2. בָּנֶיךָ
21. שֵׁנִי	12. לְהִתְרוֹצֵץ	3. גְּאֻלָה
22. תָּקִיף	13. מִינֵי	4. דַּוְקָא
	14. נָסִיךְ	5. הִבְטִיחַ
	15. סְלִיחָה	6. וְתַלְמִידַי
	16. עַמְּךָ	7. זָכַר
	17. פִּתְרוֹן	8. חַסְדֵי
	18. צִמוּקִים	9. טָעוּת

My Times

1st try _____

2nd try _____

3rd try _____

My best time:

_____

Lesson 18

GO FISH

Making the Game

There are 40 playing cards on the next five pages. Cut them out and glue them onto index cards. Or, photocopy them onto card stock and cut them out.

Playing the Game

1. Play this game with one or two friends.

2. Deal each player seven cards.

3. Put the other cards face down in the "fish" pile.

4. Take turns asking for a card that you need.

5. If your friend can give you the card you ask for, take another turn.

6. If not, "Go Fish" by taking a card from the "fish" pile. If you "catch" the "fish" you asked for, take another turn.

7. Put down on the table any complete sets of four cards.

8. The one with the most sets of four cards at the end of the game is the winner.

FOOD

חַלָה

בֵּיצָה
פֵּרוֹת
סֻכָּר

ADJECTIVES

חָכָם

יָפֶה
שָׂמֵחַ
נָמוּך

FOOD

מַצָה

בֵּיצָה
פֵּרוֹת
חָלָב

ADJECTIVES

עָצוּב

נָמוּך
יָפֶה

FOOD

פִּתָה

בֵּיצָה
פֵּרוֹת
חָלָב

ADJECTIVES

גָדוֹל

יָפֶה
שָׂמֵחַ
גָבוֹהַ

FOOD

עוּגָה

בֵּיצָה
פֵּרוֹת
חָלָב

ADJECTIVES

קָטָן

גָבוֹהַ
שָׂמֵחַ

POSITION WORDS

עַל
בְּתוֹךְ
לְיַד

POSITION WORDS

לְיַד
בְּתוֹךְ
עַל

POSITION WORDS

עַל
בְּתוֹךְ
לְיַד

POSITION WORDS

עַל
בְּתוֹךְ
לְיַד

GREETINGS

שָׁלוֹם
חַג שָׂמֵחַ
בְּרוּךְ הַבָּא
לְהִתְרָאוֹת

GREETINGS

שָׁלוֹם
חַג שָׂמֵחַ
בְּרוּךְ הַבָּא
לְהִתְרָאוֹת

GREETINGS

שָׁלוֹם
חַג שָׂמֵחַ
בְּרוּךְ הַבָּא
לְהִתְרָאוֹת

GREETINGS

שָׁלוֹם
חַג שָׂמֵחַ
בְּרוּךְ הַבָּא
לְהִתְרָאוֹת

Lesson 18

PEOPLE	CLASSROOM OBJECTS
מוֹרֶה / מוֹרָה / יֶלֶד / יַלְדָה	עִפָּרוֹן / סֵפֶר / מַחְבֶּרֶת / תַלְמִיד
תַלְמִיד / תַלְמִידָה / יֶלֶד / יַלְדָה	שֻׁלְחָן / כִּסֵּא / סֵפֶר / מַחְבֶּרֶת
מוֹרֶה / מוֹרָה / יֶלֶד / יַלְדָה	מַחְבֶּרֶת / עִפָּרוֹן / סֵפֶר / תַלְמִיד
מוֹרֶה / מוֹרָה / יֶלֶד / יַלְדָה	מַחְבֶּרֶת / עִפָּרוֹן / סֵפֶר / תַלְמִיד

Lesson 18

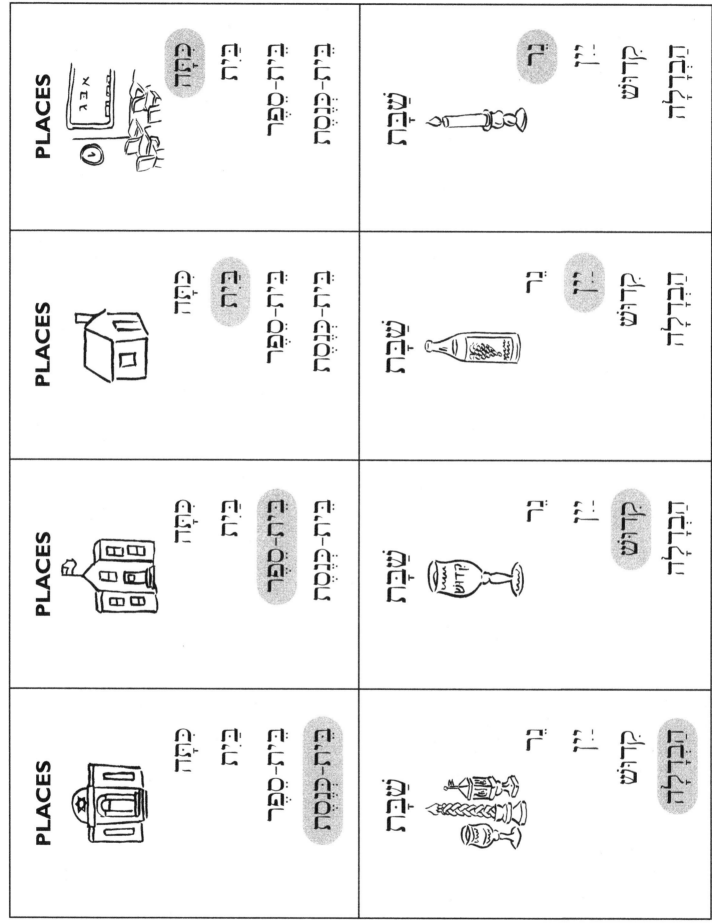

PLACES

PLACES

PLACES

PLACES

Lesson 18

ANIMALS   יִשְׂרָאֵל

ANIMALS   יִשְׂרָאֵל

ANIMALS   יִשְׂרָאֵל

ANIMALS   יִשְׂרָאֵל

Lesson 18
KEY WORDS:

מֶלֶךְ חַי

שָׁלוֹם עֲלֵיכֶם

When we sing שָׁלוֹם עֲלֵיכֶם on שַׁבָּת we welcome the angels of peace and perfection into our homes. The Hebrew word for peace and perfection is repeated many times in this song, sometimes with a ‏הַ‎ or ‏לְ‎ attached to the beginning of the word.

1. Underline the Hebrew word for "peace/perfection" each time it appears in the song below.

2. The Hebrew word מֶלֶךְ means "king" or "ruler." It comes from the ‏מ.ל.כ.‎ word family. Many other words from the ‏מ.ל.כ.‎ word family are found in this prayer. Note: The word מַלְאֲכֵי does not come from the same family. Circle all of the members of the ‏מ.ל.כ.‎ word family.

3. Practice reading this prayer.

שָׁלוֹם עֲלֵיכֶם מַלְאֲכֵי הַשָּׁרֵת מַלְאֲכֵי עֶלְיוֹן

מִמֶּלֶךְ מַלְכֵי הַמְּלָכִים הַקָּדוֹשׁ בָּרוּךְ הוּא.

בּוֹאֲכֶם לְשָׁלוֹם מַלְאֲכֵי הַשָּׁלוֹם מַלְאֲכֵי עֶלְיוֹן

מִמֶּלֶךְ מַלְכֵי הַמְּלָכִים הַקָּדוֹשׁ בָּרוּךְ הוּא.

בָּרְכוּנִי לְשָׁלוֹם מַלְאֲכֵי הַשָּׁלוֹם מַלְאֲכֵי עֶלְיוֹן

מִמֶּלֶךְ מַלְכֵי הַמְּלָכִים הַקָּדוֹשׁ בָּרוּךְ הוּא.

צֵאתְכֶם לְשָׁלוֹם מַלְאֲכֵי הַשָּׁלוֹם מַלְאֲכֵי עֶלְיוֹן

מִמֶּלֶךְ מַלְכֵי הַמְּלָכִים הַקָּדוֹשׁ בָּרוּךְ הוּא.

Lesson 18
KEY WORDS:
מֶלֶךְ חַי

LIGHTING THE חֲנֻכָּה CANDLES

Practice reading the חֲנֻכָּה candlelighting ceremony.

The following two בְּרָכוֹת are said each night before lighting the candles:

בָּרוּךְ אַתָּה יְיָ אֱלֹהֵינוּ מֶלֶךְ הָעוֹלָם,

אֲשֶׁר קִדְּשָׁנוּ בְּמִצְוֹתָיו וְצִוָּנוּ לְהַדְלִיק נֵר שֶׁל חֲנֻכָּה.

בָּרוּךְ אַתָּה יְיָ אֱלֹהֵינוּ מֶלֶךְ הָעוֹלָם,

שֶׁעָשָׂה נִסִּים לַאֲבוֹתֵינוּ בַּיָּמִים הַהֵם בַּזְּמַן הַזֶּה.

The following בְּרָכָה is said after lighting the candles on the first night only:

בָּרוּךְ אַתָּה יְיָ אֱלֹהֵינוּ מֶלֶךְ הָעוֹלָם,

שֶׁהֶחֱיָנוּ וְקִיְּמָנוּ וְהִגִּיעָנוּ לַזְּמַן הַזֶּה.

While lighting the candles, the following passage can be said. Practice reading it.

הַנֵּרוֹת הַלָּלוּ אֲנַחְנוּ מַדְלִיקִין עַל הַנִּסִּים וְעַל

הַנִּפְלָאוֹת וְעַל הַתְּשׁוּעוֹת וְעַל הַמִּלְחָמוֹת,

שֶׁעָשִׂיתָ לַאֲבוֹתֵינוּ בַּיָּמִים הָהֵם בַּזְּמַן הַזֶּה.

After lighting the candles, we sing this well-known song. Read it or sing it.

מָעוֹז צוּר יְשׁוּעָתִי, לְךָ נָאֶה לְשַׁבֵּחַ.

תִּכּוֹן בֵּית תְּפִלָּתִי, וְשָׁם תּוֹדָה נְזַבֵּחַ.

לְעֵת תָּכִין מַטְבֵּחַ, מִצָּר הַמְנַבֵּחַ.

אָז אֶגְמֹר, בְּשִׁיר מִזְמוֹר, חֲנֻכַּת הַמִּזְבֵּחַ.

72

Lesson 19

KEY WORDS:
בְּכָל נַפְשְׁךָ

מַה נִשְׁתַּנָה

On פֶּסַח at the סֵדֶר the youngest child usually asks the Four Questions. You are now able to read them in Hebrew. In the words שֶׁבְּכָל and מִכָּל the ָ is pronounced as וֹ. Highlight these words in yellow each time they appear below. Practice reading or singing the Four Questions.

מַה נִשְׁתַּנָה הַלַּיְלָה הַזֶּה מִכָּל הַלֵּילוֹת?

שֶׁבְּכָל הַלֵּילוֹת אָנוּ אוֹכְלִין חָמֵץ וּמַצָּה,

הַלַּיְלָה הַזֶּה כֻּלוֹ מַצָּה.

שֶׁבְּכָל הַלֵּילוֹת אָנוּ אוֹכְלִין שְׁאָר יְרָקוֹת,

הַלַּיְלָה הַזֶּה מָרוֹר.

שֶׁבְּכָל הַלֵּילוֹת אֵין אָנוּ מַטְבִּילִין אֲפִילוּ פַּעַם אֶחָת,

הַלַּיְלָה הַזֶּה שְׁתֵּי פְעָמִים.

שֶׁבְּכָל הַלֵּילוֹת אָנוּ אוֹכְלִין בֵּין יוֹשְׁבִין וּבֵין מְסֻבִּין,

הַלַּיְלָה הַזֶּה כֻּלָנוּ מְסֻבִּין.

Lesson 19

מַה־טֹבוּ

It is customary to say the following בְּרָכָה whenever we study important Jewish texts. In this בְּרָכָה we thank God for the chance to be learning words of Torah.

בָּרוּךְ אַתָּה יְיָ אֱלֹהֵינוּ מֶלֶךְ הָעוֹלָם,

אֲשֶׁר קִדְּשָׁנוּ בְּמִצְוֹתָיו וְצִוָּנוּ לַעֲסוֹק בְּדִבְרֵי תוֹרָה.

The passage that follows comes from the Torah. It can be found in the book of Numbers. It tells the story of Balak and Bilam.

As the Children of Israel got close to the Land of Israel, they defeated many powerful kings. Balak, the king of Moab, grew frightened when he heard about the Israelites and their victories. He sent for the prophet Bilam and asked him to curse the Israelites.

At first, Bilam did not want to go, but King Balak insisted. On his journey to Moab, an angel appeared in the middle of the road. The angel was invisible to Bilam, but his donkey could see it. The donkey stopped and refused to go on, even after Bilam beat her. Finally, the donkey spoke to Bilam and told him about the angel. The angel ordered Bilam to say only what God told him to say.

Bilam followed Balak up a hill that looked out over the Israelite camp. Balak ordered Bilam to curse the Israelites, but whenever Bilam opened his mouth, only a blessing came out. He said:

מַה־טֹבוּ אֹהָלֶיךָ יַעֲקֹב, מִשְׁכְּנֹתֶיךָ יִשְׂרָאֵל.

"How good are your tents, O Jacob, your dwelling places O Israel."

Today, we often say this prayer when we enter a synagogue, and it has become the first prayer in the morning service.

1. Practice reading this prayer.
2. Circle the two names for Jacob that it contains.

Lesson 19

בְּכָל נַפְשְׁךָ

לְכָה דוֹדִי

The Talmud tells us that at sunset on שַׁבָּת eve, Rabbi Hanina used to dress in his finest robes and say, "Come! Let us go out to welcome שַׁבָּת the Queen." Rabbi Yanai would put on his best שַׁבָּת robes and say, "Come, שַׁבָּת, O bride." The prayer לְכָה דוֹדִי was written for the beginning of the שַׁבָּת evening service. The author of לְכָה דוֹדִי based this prayer on the story from the Talmud.

1. Practice reading or singing this wonderful prayer. Remember: In the word וּבְצָהֳלָה (on line 8) the ◌ָ and the first ◌ָ are pronounced as וֹ.

2. The Hebrew word כַּלָה means "bride." Circle the word כַּלָה or כַּלָה every time it appears.

1. לְכָה דוֹדִי לִקְרַאת כַּלָה, פְּנֵי שַׁבָּת נְקַבְּלָה.

2. שָׁמוֹר וְזָכוֹר בְּדִבּוּר אֶחָד, הִשְׁמִיעָנוּ אֵל הַמְיֻחָד.

3. יְיָ אֶחָד וּשְׁמוֹ אֶחָד, לְשֵׁם וּלְתִפְאֶרֶת וְלִתְהִלָה.

4. לְכָה דוֹדִי לִקְרַאת כַּלָה, פְּנֵי שַׁבָּת נְקַבְּלָה.

5. לִקְרַאת שַׁבָּת לְכוּ וְנֵלְכָה, כִּי הִיא מְקוֹר הַבְּרָכָה.

6. מֵרֹאשׁ מִקֶּדֶם נְסוּכָה, סוֹף מַעֲשֶׂה בְּמַחֲשָׁבָה תְּחִלָה.

7. לְכָה דוֹדִי לִקְרַאת כַּלָה, פְּנֵי שַׁבָּת נְקַבְּלָה.

8. בּוֹאִי בְשָׁלוֹם עֲטֶרֶת בַּעֲלָה, גַּם בְּשִׂמְחָה וּבְצָהֳלָה,

9. תּוֹךְ אֱמוּנֵי עַם סְגֻלָה, בּוֹאִי כַלָה! בּוֹאִי כַלָה!

Lesson 20

KEY WORDS:

מֹשֶׁה גּוֹי

שְׁמַע וְאָהַבְתָּ

The שְׁמַע and וְאָהַבְתָּ come from the תּוֹרָה. They are found in a מְזוּזָה and in תְּפִילִין handwritten on parchment. The שְׁמַע makes the most important Jewish statement: "Hear O Israel, Adonai is our God, Adonai is One." The Key Words for Lesson 19, בְּכָל נַפְשְׁךָ, come from the וְאָהַבְתָּ. We are told to love God with all our heart, all our soul, and all our might. The שְׁמַע and וְאָהַבְתָּ can also be found in the סִדּוּר because they are a very important part of the Jewish worship service.

1. Draw a box around the Key Words בְּכָל נַפְשְׁךָ in the prayer below.
2. Circle all the words that have two ▪ ▪ vowels next to each other.
3. In the words וּבְכָל and בְּכָל the ▪ sounds like וֹ. Highlight these vowels in yellow.
4. Practice reading the שְׁמַע and וְאָהַבְתָּ prayers.
5. Extra Activity: Ask an adult to show you a מְזוּזָה parchment. How much of the מְזוּזָה can you read without vowels?

שְׁמַע יִשְׂרָאֵל יְיָ אֱלֹהֵינוּ יְיָ אֶחָד.

וְאָהַבְתָּ אֵת יְיָ אֱלֹהֶיךָ בְּכָל־לְבָבְךָ וּבְכָל־נַפְשְׁךָ וּבְכָל־מְאֹדֶךָ.

וְהָיוּ הַדְּבָרִים הָאֵלֶּה אֲשֶׁר אָנֹכִי מְצַוְּךָ הַיּוֹם עַל־לְבָבֶךָ. וְשִׁנַּנְתָּם לְבָנֶיךָ וְדִבַּרְתָּ בָּם בְּשִׁבְתְּךָ בְּבֵיתֶךָ וּבְלֶכְתְּךָ בַדֶּרֶךְ וּבְשָׁכְבְּךָ וּבְקוּמֶךָ. וּקְשַׁרְתָּם לְאוֹת עַל־יָדֶךָ וְהָיוּ לְטֹטָפֹת בֵּין עֵינֶיךָ. וּכְתַבְתָּם עַל־מְזֻזוֹת בֵּיתֶךָ וּבִשְׁעָרֶיךָ.

In some congregations, the following lines are said silently.
In other congregations, these lines are read or chanted out loud.

לְמַעַן תִּזְכְּרוּ וַעֲשִׂיתֶם אֶת כָּל מִצְוֹתָי וִהְיִיתֶם קְדֹשִׁים לֵאלֹהֵיכֶם.

אֲנִי יְיָ אֱלֹהֵיכֶם אֲשֶׁר הוֹצֵאתִי אֶתְכֶם מֵאֶרֶץ מִצְרַיִם לִהְיוֹת לָכֶם לֵאלֹהִים. אֲנִי יְיָ אֱלֹהֵיכֶם.

BLESSINGS FOR READING THE תּוֹרָה

The תּוֹרָה is the first five books in the Bible. The תּוֹרָה is read in the בֵּית-כְּנֶסֶת on שַׁבָּת and holidays. In traditional congregations it is also read on Mondays and Thursdays. Before the תּוֹרָה is read, a special בְּרָכָה is said. A second בְּרָכָה is said after the תּוֹרָה is read. Both of these בְּרָכוֹת bless God for giving us the תּוֹרָה. Practice reading both בְּרָכוֹת below.

בָּרְכוּ אֶת יְיָ הַמְבֹרָךְ. בָּרוּךְ יְיָ הַמְבֹרָךְ לְעוֹלָם וָעֶד.
בָּרוּךְ אַתָּה יְיָ אֱלֹהֵינוּ מֶלֶךְ הָעוֹלָם אֲשֶׁר בָּחַר בָּנוּ
מִכָּל הָעַמִּים וְנָתַן לָנוּ אֶת תּוֹרָתוֹ. בָּרוּךְ אַתָּה יְיָ
נוֹתֵן הַתּוֹרָה.

בָּרוּךְ אַתָּה יְיָ אֱלֹהֵינוּ מֶלֶךְ הָעוֹלָם אֲשֶׁר נָתַן לָנוּ
תּוֹרַת אֱמֶת וְחַיֵּי עוֹלָם נָטַע בְּתוֹכֵנוּ. בָּרוּךְ אַתָּה יְיָ
נוֹתֵן הַתּוֹרָה.

Lesson 20

גּוֹי   מֹשֶׁה

בְּרֵאשִׁית

Every year on שִׂמְחַת תּוֹרָה, we start reading the תּוֹרָה from
the beginning. These first verses tell how God created the world.
Read the first three verses from the תּוֹרָה. Circle the word that
means "the water" and the word that means "on."

בְּרֵאשִׁית בָּרָא אֱלֹהִים אֵת הַשָּׁמַיִם וְאֵת הָאָרֶץ: וְהָאָרֶץ
הָיְתָה תֹהוּ וָבֹהוּ וְחֹשֶׁךְ עַל־פְּנֵי תְהוֹם וְרוּחַ אֱלֹהִים
מְרַחֶפֶת עַל־פְּנֵי הַמָּיִם: וַיֹּאמֶר אֱלֹהִים יְהִי אוֹר וַיְהִי־אוֹר:

When these verses are printed in a book, accent marks
(called "trope") are added to show the reader the correct
melody to chant. Read these verses again, as they are written
below. Just ignore the accent marks and any extra dots.

בְּרֵאשִׁ֖ית בָּרָ֣א אֱלֹהִ֑ים אֵ֥ת הַשָּׁמַ֖יִם וְאֵ֥ת הָאָֽרֶץ: וְהָאָ֗רֶץ
הָיְתָ֥ה תֹ֙הוּ֙ וָבֹ֔הוּ וְחֹ֖שֶׁךְ עַל־פְּנֵ֣י תְה֑וֹם וְר֣וּחַ אֱלֹהִ֔ים
מְרַחֶ֖פֶת עַל־פְּנֵ֥י הַמָּֽיִם: וַיֹּ֥אמֶר אֱלֹהִ֖ים יְהִ֣י א֑וֹר וַֽיְהִי־אֽוֹר:

The actual תּוֹרָה scroll is written without vowels. Here are the
same verses as they appear in the Torah. Can you read them?

בראשית ברא אלהים את השמים ואת הארץ והארץ
היתה תהו ובהו וחשך על־פני תהום ורוח אלהים
מרחפת על־פני המים ויאמר אלהים יהי אור ויהי־אור

KEY WORD MEMORY

Play the game *Memory* with one or two friends.

1. Cut out the cards on this page and on the next two pages.
2. Mix up the cards and put them face down on the table in neat rows.
3. Take turns picking two Key Word cards. Try to find a Hebrew word card and its matching English word card.
4. If they match, keep the cards and take another turn.
5. If the cards don't match, put them back face down in the same place.
6. The one with the most matching pairs at the end wins.

Passover	פֶּסַח	**commandment**	מִצְוָה
Sabbath	שַׁבָּת	**fish**	דָּג
mother	אִמָּא	**father**	אַבָּא
Passover "bread"	מַצָּה	**Passover book**	הַגָּדָה

Hebrew	עִבְרִית	hand	יָד
classroom	כִּתָּה	blessing for wine	קִדּוּשׁ
Israel	יִשְׂרָאֵל	holiday of costumes	פּוּרִים
first Hebrew letter	אָלֶף	commandments	מִצְוֹת
good morning	בֹּקֶר טוֹב	I	אֲנִי
happy holiday	חַג שָׂמֵחַ	wine	יַיִן
please, you're welcome	בְּבַקָּשָׁה	Sabbath bread	חַלָה

congratulations	מַזָל טוֹב	tree of life	עֵץ חַיִּים
sorry	סְלִיחָה	table	שֻׁלְחָן
synagogue	בֵּית-כְּנֶסֶת	alive (=18)	חַי
blessing	בְּרָכָה	Moses	מֹשֶׁה
king	מֶלֶךְ	end of שַׁבָּת	הַבְדָּלָה
with all your soul	בְּכָל נַפְשְׁךָ	book	סֵפֶר
nation	גּוֹי	peace, perfection	שָׁלוֹם

WRITING SCRIPT

English is written in block letters or in script. Hebrew, as you know, is written in block letters, and it can also be written in script. Hebrew script is easy to learn and fun to write. Just practice writing the script letters, Key Words, and vocabulary that follow. Read each letter or word out loud, then practice writing it. Use these pages after you complete Lesson 20 in זְמַן לִקְרֹא.

ו שׁ י

דְּ זִין

ה ס

תְּ ר

חַ חַיִּים ח

תַּחַת תַּחַת

תּוֹרָה תּוֹרָה

בָ בָּ ב

רַבִּי רַבִּי

בַּיִת בַּיִת

כ כְּ כ ____ כ כ כ ____ ד כְּ

כֵּן כֵּן כֵן

ז כ ק קֵ ק

זִבְרָה צֶבְרָה צֶבְרָה

פ פַּ פ פַּ פ פ

ם סַ ם

כֻּתָּה כֻּתָּה כֻּתָּה

אֵיפֹה אֵיפֹה אֵיפֹה

בְּרָכָה בְּרָכָה בְּרָכָה

סֵפֶר סֵפֶר סֵפֶר

בֵּית-סֵפֶר בֵּית-סֵפֶר בֵּית-סֵפֶר

פֶּסַח פֶּסַח פֶּסַח _____

פּוּרִים פּוּרִים פּוּרִים _____

ד פ֚ ע֚ צ֚ _____

יָד יָּד עַם צַא צַא _____

עִבְרִית עִבְרִית עִבְרִית _____

עֶפְרוֹן עֶפְרוֹן עֶפְרוֹן _____

מ N N֚ _____

מִי אֵי אֵי מָה אַה אַה _____

מַיִם אַיִם אַיִם _____

מוֹרָה אוֹרָה אוֹרָה _____

מוֹרָה אוֹרָה אוֹרָה _____

מַחְבֶּרֶת אַחְבֶּרֶת אַחְבֶּרֶת

צ 3

מַצָה אַצְוָה אַצְוָה

צְדָקָה צְדָקָה צְדָקָה

מִצְוָה מִצְוָה מִצְוָה

בַּר-מִצְוָה בַּר-מִצְוָה

בַּת-מִצְוָה בַּת-מִצְוָה

א אָן אָן אַבָּא אָבָּא אָבָּא אָבָּא

אִמָא אִמָא אִמָא אִמָא

אַתָה אַתָה אַתָה אַת אָת אָת

כִּסֵא כִּסֵא כִּסֵא

אוֹהֵב אוֹהֵב אוֹהֵב

אוֹהֶבֶת _____ אוהבת _____ אוהבת

גַ _____ ג ג

דָג _____ דָּג דָּג

גּוֹי _____ גּוֹי גּוֹי _____ גִּיר גִּיר גִּיר

מָגֵן דָוִד _____ מָגֵן דָּוִד מָגֵן דָּוִד

הַגָּדָה _____ הַגָּדָה הַגָּדָה

ט _____ ט ט

קָטָן _____ קָטָן קָטָן

טוֹב _____ טוֹב טוֹב

בֹּקֶר טוֹב _____ בֹּקֶר טוֹב בֹּקֶר טוֹב

נ _____ נ נ _____ אֲנִי אֲנִי אֲנִי

נֵר _____ נֵר _____

בֵּית־כְּנֶסֶת בֵּית־כְּנֶסֶת בֵּית־כְּנֶסֶת _____

שׁ שֶׁ _____ שׁ שֶׁ שׁ _____

שַׁבָּת שַׁבָּת שַׁבָּת _____

מֹשֶׁה מֹשֶׁה _____

קָדוֹשׁ קָדוֹשׁ קָדוֹשׁ _____

בְּבַקָשָׁה בְּבַקָשָׁה בְּבַקָשָׁה _____

חַג שָׂמֵחַ חַג שָׂמֵחַ חַג שָׂמֵחַ _____

מִשְׁפָּחָה מִשְׁפָּחָה מִשְׁפָּחָה _____

ל ל _____ לֹא לֹא לֹא _____

עַל עַל _____ עַל־יָד עַל־יָד עַל־יָד _____

דֶּגֶל   דֶּגֶל   דֶּגֶל

יֶלֶד   יֶלֶד   יֶלֶד

יַלְדָּה   יַלְדָּה   יַלְדָּה

חַלָּה   חַלָּה   חַלָּה

כֶּלֶב   כֶּלֶב   כֶּלֶב

לוּחַ   לוּחַ   לוּחַ

הַבְדָּלָה   הַבְדָּלָה   הַבְדָּלָה

לוֹמֵד   לוֹמֵד   לוֹמֵד

לוֹמֶדֶת   לוֹמֶדֶת   לוֹמֶדֶת

גָּדוֹל   גָּדוֹל   גָּדוֹל

שָׁלוֹם   שָׁלוֹם   שָׁלוֹם

WRITING SCRIPT

יִשְׂרָאֵל   יִשְׂרָאֵל   _____

סְלִיחָה   סְלִיחָה   _____

חָתוּל   חָתוּל   _____

מַזָּל טוֹב   מַזָּל טוֹב   _____

שֻׁלְחָן   שֻׁלְחָן   _____

מֶלֶךְ   מֶלֶךְ   _____

בְּכָל נַפְשְׁךָ   בְּכָל נַפְשְׁךָ   _____

ךְ   ךְ   _____

עֵץ חַיִּים   עֵץ חַיִּים   _____

ף   ף   _____

אָלֶף   אָלֶף   _____

WRITING SCRIPT

WRITING SCRIPT